How To Reach The Masses

Seasoned Pastors Expound on the Seven Pillars

William E. Thrasher., Jr.

Copyright 2023 by William E. Thrasher., Jr.

All rights reserved. This book or any portion thereof may not be reproduced or used in any manner whatsoever without the express written permission of the publisher except for the use of brief quotation in a book review.

Inquiries and Book Orders should be addressed to:

Great Writers Media
Email: info@greatwritersmedia.com
Phone: 877-600-5469

ISBN: 978-1-960939-78-4 (sc)
ISBN: 978-1-960939-93-7 (hc)
ISBN: 978-1-960939-79-1 (ebk)

Contents

Dedication 5
Special Thanks.. 7
How to Reach the Masses... 9
Foreword... 13
Pillar 1: Church Administation 15
Pillar 2: Christian Education as a Foundational
and Supporting Member 18
Pillar 3: Parishioner Welfare 24
Pillar 4: Stewardship.. 30
Pillar 5: Temple Maintenance 33
Pillar 6: Christian Fellowship 45
Pillar 7: The Ministry of Worship 59

Advent of Technology 66

Dedication

THIS BOOK IS DEDICATED TO all the first time pastors who will answer the call to the great commission and strive to reach the masses I pray you will .find this little book to be a source of spiritual guidance.

Special Thanks

I wish to thank my fellow pastors who have so willingly and graciously consented to contribute to this book. Without their support this book would not be possible.

How to Reach the Masses
Seven Pastors Expound on the Seven Pillars

The original book *Seven Pillars for Successful Service* was born out of my own experience as a first-time pastor who was trying to figure out where to start and what made sense. I knew that fulfilling the great Commission was the ultimate goal, but I was somewhat overwhelmed as to how best to proceed.

I was blessed to have some very good mentors who were willing to give me guidance and provided me with the benefit of their years of experience and wisdom. But the reality was they were busy pastors just like me and, as helpful as they were, there was still much that I needed to figure out on my own.

Seven Pillars for Successful Service is the fruit of mentoring, laboring, and most importantly the guidance of the Holy Spirit. This work was never intended to be the last word on this subject. It was however designed to help first-time pastors and developing churches get a better focus on the fundamental areas that any effective ministry should be focused on as they build their ministry. The Seven Pillars are:

Pillar 1: Church Administration
Pillar 2: Christian Education
Pillar 3: Parishioner Welfare
Pillar 4: Stewardship
Pillar 5: Temple Maintenance
Pillar 6: Christian Fellowship
Pillar 7: Ministry of Worship

When I began writing the initial manuscript for *Seven Pillars,* I did not have the slightest thought that a global pandemic was even possible. The devastating toll of this viral menace is yet to be comprehended. Its impact on the religious community has been widespread and has caused a paradigm shift of incalculable proportions. The notion that things will return to normal, where churches can conduct worship and all other ministerial functions as before is still doubtful for the near future. This begs the question: how do we reach the masses post- pandemic? Are the Seven Pillars still relevant, and if so how can we continue to build upon them? The goal as well as the vision of this latest work is to answer these questions and provide an additional bonus on how today's technology can be an effective tool in reaching the masses.

Assembled here is the collective wisdom of eight seasoned pastors (seven addressing the Pillars and one addressing technology) who have graciously offered their insight on the Seven Pillars. First-time pastors are offered the chance to get firsthand knowledge born from these pastors' "trial by fire" experience. There is no need to re-invent the wheel when the spiritual unction provided by these seasoned pastors is at your disposal.

This latest work is by no means a substitute for formal training, but if that is not possible, the information presented here can be a vital tool in helping to undergird your ministerial journey.

Not every church is going to be a mega church, but every church can have a mega impact on the community that it serves by making sure that your church understands how best to utilize the knowledge of the Seven Pillars.

Finally, if this book does no more than challenge you to compare your current ministerial path with what is presented here, then we believe that our work has been accomplished. It is our prayer that our Heavenly Father will richly bless you and your ministry with the spiritual wherewithal necessary to reach the masses and fulfill His great commission.

Foreword

WHERE IN THE WORLD WAS William Thrasher, Jr. when I was a new pastor starting out in ministry? If someone would have given me or told me about a book called *The Seven Pillars for Successful Service*, there were a lot of mistakes I did not have to make and there were a lot of nights I could have gone to sleep earlier! Consequently, as a new pastor trying to do it all on my own, I made a lot of mistakes with ministry decisions and spent a lot of sleepless nights because of those decisions! And I assure those of you who are first-time pastors reading this Foreword that you could certainly say AMEN!

In his first printing of his book, Pastor Thrasher gave all first time or new pastors Seven Pillars or building blocks that all pastors must deal with at some point in their ministry. Topics like Church Administration, Christian Education, Parishioner Welfare, Stewardship, Temple Maintenance, Christian Fellowship, and Ministry of Worship gave critical information that would assist any pastor starting out in ministry. Each brief chapter gave pastors information that they could use for the life of their ministry. The book alone was a wealth of knowledge for any pastor or church leadership.

However, Pastor Thrasher was not finished. In the sequel, *How to Reach the Masses: Seasoned Pastors Expound on the Seven Pillars*, he asked some of his pastor friends to give their personal input and comments on these Seven Pillars, in their own words. As an incredible bonus to this book, Pastor Thrasher has added an eighth pillar on Technology, which exploded in churches across America during the Coronavirus pandemic. Churches who never used technology before were forced to use Facebook, YouTube, or some other type of social media to keep in touch with the members of their congregation. Thank you, Pastor Thrasher, for adding this eighth pillar that new pastors *must* apply to their ministries, because Technology is here to stay.

If you are a new pastor, make sure that you read and apply this book in your ministry. I assure you it will benefit you for many years to come. If you are not a new pastor, purchase this book and give it to a new pastor. I promise you they will thank you for investing in their life and their ministry.

Fred Luter, Jr.
Pastor, Franklin Avenue Baptist Church, New Orleans, LA.
Former President of the Southern Baptist Convention

PILLAR 1

Church Administation

A Definition Of Church Administration
By Rev. Dr. Carlton Caldwell

CHURCH IS OF GOD. AND when it comes to church administration, there are certain characteristics that are intrinsic to its very nature. First, the word "church" in the New Testament comes from the Greek word *ekklesia*. It comes from a root word made up of the preposition *ek* (out of) and a verb *kaleo* (to be called). *Ekklesia* means "to call out of." So, Church, *ekklesia*, are those who have been called out from the world to His marvelous light. Church is those who have been called out from sin to salvation. The church is a living community of people redeemed by Jesus Christ. They have been touched by their Lord. They are set apart for Him and for His service. They are a distinctive people on a mission for their Lord in this world.

"Administration" used as a noun is the process or activity of running a business, organization, or even a church.

Administration equips the church to do the work of the church in a *coherent* and *comprehensive* manner. It provides guidance as church leaders implement spiritual, human, physical, and financial resources to achieve ecumenical goals and objectives.

Church Leaders In Church Administration

The chief biblical texts that underscore the requirements of church leaders are 1 Timothy 3:1-13, 2 Timothy 2:1-13, Titus 1:5-9, Acts 6:1-6, and Exodus 18:21-22. The qualifications spelled out in these passages can be summarized in four words:

1. *Commitments.* Clearly church leaders should be committed to Jesus Christ as Savior and Lord.
2. *Conviction.* Clearly church leaders should have strong conviction as to God's identity and the nature of the church.
3. *Competency.* You cannot bypass the need for godly leadership and receive God's blessing. There must be holy men and women who are in positions of responsibility within a church; there is no substitute for that. Paul repeatedly said that Christ is the head of the church (1 Cor. 11:3; Eph. 1:22; 4:15; 5:23; Col. 1:18). As its head, Christ wants to rule His church through holy people. Unholy people serve only to obfuscate and obstruct. Satan and Christ don't cooperate.

    It's amazing how most churches choose their leadership, especially in the Black church. We select people who are the most successful in business, who have the most to say, and who have the most money.

A man or woman should not be a leader in the church because he/she is a successful in business, has innate leadership ability, or is a supersalesman. He or she should be a leader because they are a person of God.
4. *Character.* The greatest of the four qualifications for leadership is character. Does the person possess self-control, hospitality, gentleness (control of anger), a quest for holiness, temperance? Is there a history of greed, manipulation, or self-centeredness? Are they faithful to their spouse?

The key to church administration is that we assume that all who work in the church are engaged in ministry. Pastors, deacons, and heads of auxiliaries should all be engaged in ministry. Since the deacons and heads of the auxiliaries are the primary support base of the pastor, it is important that the pastor envision the ministry and work with the deacons and heads of auxiliaries to define the tasks to be accomplished and see to it that the resources are provided to accomplish the task. This requires planning, setting functional goals and objectives, and organization. The pastor should define the direction, set priorities, assign tasks, evaluate performances, and set the tone for the church to accomplish the vision.

In closing, since the church is of God, it must be understood that Jesus is the head of the church (see my organizational chart) and the reason for its existence is to please God and not people. Likewise, church administrative policies and procedures are of God in that they provide guided, adequate instructions that will result in God being glorified, loved, and therefore worshiped.

PILLAR 2

Christian Education as a Foundational and Supporting Member

By Rev. Dr. C. Dennis Edward

THE NEW OXFORD AMERICAN DICTIONARY defines ecclesiology as "theology as applied to the nature and structure of the Christian church." The study of ecclesiology presents several metaphors for our consideration, two of which claim our attention in this writing: the concepts of being both a human body and a building. Both require a structural system for support. Additionally, both will remain erect because of these unique systems and, conversely, both would collapse without them.

Because of these supporting systems, both possess the potential for further development or enlargement. Two means of broadening show up in the aforementioned metaphors. The apostle Paul uses both in his depiction of the church where he says it is *"built upon the foundation of the apostles and prophets, Jesus Christ himself being the chief corner stone; in whom all the building fitly framed together growth unto an holy temple in the Lord"* (Ephesians 2:20, 21 KJV). The terms used for broadening are *epoikodomeo [Gr., build upon, to build up, as placing one brick upon another]* and *auxano [Gr., to expand, to increase like a plant or an infant].* Again, in his first letter to the church at Corinth, the apostle refers to the church as a body: *"Now ye are the body of Christ and members in particular"* (12:27 KJV). The structural components of the spiritual house are referred to as living stones which are built up as a spiritual house [ref. 1 Peter 4:2]. Both terms are appropriate and congruent in that the church and its individual components possess the dynamism of life. Both the building and the body are living and the ultimate for both is increase, expansion, extension, and augmentation. The church as both a living organism and a living construct with their individual components or members have the potential and resident quality of growth. The church and her members (living, functioning parts) are made to grow. E. Stanley Jones, in his book, *Growing Spiritually* said, "The creative God made [us] for creative growth. Growth is the law of [our] being. Violate that law, and you violate yourself."[1] Growth is an essentiality of life.

Growth is not only essential and expected but endless. Throughout all spiritual life, there is to be expansion. The promise of that is secured in the words of the apostle, "…

---

[1] E. Stanley Jones, *"Growing Spiritually,"* (Abingdon Press: Nashville, TN) p. 1

He who began a good work in you will bring it to completion at the day of Jesus Christ" [Philippians 1:6 ESV]. The fact of its continuance is evidence that growth (increase) has not yet reached its full development from a simpler to a more complex stage, or to its ultimate state of being. Growth itself is both an injunction and an action. It is what has been ordered and is the resultant aggrandizement. What is that inciter, that stimulus for growth?

For the church, it is Christian education. Education itself has been defined as an ongoing pedagogical process and experience where there is facilitating and acquisition of knowledge, skills, values, morals, beliefs, and habits. Christian Education Ministries defines Christian education as "a reverent attempt to discover the divinely ordained process by which individuals grow toward Christ-likeness, and to work with that process. That is to say that Christian education is concerned with growing persons."[2] By this process they are transformed and inculcated with the person of Jesus Christ, his life, and his teachings.

Christian education is transformative. Its objective is to instill growing persons with an understanding and appreciation of the personality, life, and teachings of Jesus and to lead them to better personal experiences. Another is to foster in growing persons a progressive and continuous development of Christian (Christ-like) qualities of character and comportment. At the same time, other objectives are: to motivate; to stimulate to action; to constrain; to enable and equip. Christian education helps people, as Jerry Stubblefield said,

---

[2] CEM (internet definition)

to recognize their own spiritual needs, values, and objectives, and then facilitate growth in these vital areas.[3]

Teaching was the hallmark of the ministry of Jesus. One of the first acts of his earthly ministry was to *"ordain twelve that they should be with him…"* (Mark 3:14). They were separated unto him that they might be taught and trained by him and that he might prepare them to teach and to train others—an ongoing ministry. It was not occasional, but structured, intentional, and intensive. It was at the center of his works. The Gospel of Matthew recorded: *"And seeing the multitudes, he went up into a mountain and when he was set, his disciples came unto him: and he opened his mouth and taught them…"* (5:1 KJV). These disciples would be transformed by the education ministry of Jesus. They were before, as Kendrick Strong described them, "closed-minded, self-centered, distrustful, fearful, and skeptical," [but] Jesus taught those disciples basic lessons to hasten their spiritual maturity, lessons which ultimately took root and came to flower."[4] This process of teaching and training these disciples was three and a half years in the making. During that time, the disciples of Christ became veritable witnesses of the words and works of Christ, later boldly proclaiming, *"That which we have both seen and heard declare we unto you…"* (1 John 1:3). Their educational experience was so impactful that the transformed disciples, facing harsh scrutiny and threats, would unflinchingly declare, *"We are unable to stop speaking about what we have seen and heard"* (Acts 4:20 HCSB). Their

---

[3] Jerry M. Stubblefield, *"The Effective Minister of Christian Education,"* (Broadman and Holman Publishers: Nashville, TN) p. 10

[4] Kendrick Strong, *"All the Master's Men,"* (Christian Herald Books: Chappaqua, NY) p. 15

senses were awakened, and they were like "children born into a new world, whose first and by no means least important course of lessons consists in the uses of their senses in observing the wonderful objects by which they were surrounded."[5]

In like manner, those born of the Lord are awakened to a new life. Eyes once blinded now see. Ears once deaf now hear. Their spiritual senses are titillated by a desire to learn and to grow (1 Peter 2:2). Christian education is vitally important to that growth, so vital that Matthew 19:20 recorded the last words of our Lord to his followers: "...*teaching* [instructing, imparting knowledge to, explaining to] *them to observe* [watch, or guard, or keep] *everything I have commanded you*" (brackets mine). So indispensable is Christian education that the apostle Paul said that the Lord gifted the church with teachers (Ephesian 4:11-16). Ralph Cottrell lists three immediate goals and three ultimate goals of the teacher (Christian education) from this passage:

Immediate Goals:

- a) The Perfecting of the Saints: to equip, to completely furnish the saints
- b) The Work of the Ministry: the combined efforts of those who are engaged in serving or attending those reached with the Gospel

---

[5] A. B. Bruce, *"The Training of The Twelve,"* (Kregel Publications: Grand Rapids, MI) p.41

c) To edify or build up the body of Christ, the result of attaining the first two goals

The Ultimate Goals:

a) That We Should All Reach Unity in the Faith: oneness, agreement among teachers and other concerned Christians concerning the Word of God
b) That All Should Attain the Highest Knowledge of Jesus: to know Christ fully and to have the privilege of introducing others to Him.
c) That We All Should Be Fully Developed Christians: to be mature, fully developed followers of the Lord Jesus Christ[6]

Christian education, lastly, is at the inception, the base of Christian life in the church: *"Faith comes by hearing and hearing by the word of God."* By education, people are transformed from being children of the darkness to children of the light. God uses it to form them into the image of his Son. In addition, it is the means by which saints are sustained in maturation and are stabilized and steadied in the truth.

---

[6] Ralph Cottrell, *"Go Ye…and Teach,"* (Baker Book House: Grand Rapids, MI) pgs. 17-22

PILLAR 3

Parishioner Welfare

By Rev. Ralph Blanks

I SERVED IN THE UNITED Methodist Church for over thirty years, and since 2017 have pastored in the Baptist Church. Within the African Methodist Episcopal Church, parishioner welfare is referred to as **pastoral care or Class System**. Parishioner welfare is carried out through a partnership between the pastor and the Deacons' ministry. Regardless of the name, the focus is the same across denominations: to foster a close-knit, warm church family that cares, attends, encourages, and communicates. Parishioner welfare requires keeping the pastor apprised of those who are sick, in the hospital, in need of special prayer, or of a visit due to a significant life event such as the birth of a child, a wedding anniversary, birthday, or a death. *Let us be concerned for one another, to help one another to show love and to do good. Let us not give up the habit of meeting together...*

.Instead, let us encourage one another all the more... Hebrews 10:24-25 GNT

The ministry of pastoral care is based upon the ministry of Jesus as the Good Shepherd. *I am the good shepherd. The good shepherd lays down his life for the sheep... I am the good shepherd; I know my sheep and my sheep know me. John 10-11-14 NIV.* He takes care of His people through you, the pastor. As the pastor, you are to care for your church in a way that reflects Jesus' care. You are an "under-shepherd" whom God has called to lead His people. *Be shepherds of God's flock that is under your care, watching over them - not because you must, but because you are willing, as God wants you to be; not pursing dishonest gain, but eager to serve....I Peter 5:2 NIV* Your church, whether mega, small, or historic, is the living body of Jesus Christ in the world today and was created by Almighty God to be a family of sisters and brothers in Christ who encourage and support one another to live and love like Jesus Christ.

In the Baptist Church Covenant, we commit **to watch over one another in brotherly love; to remember one another in prayer; to aid one another in sickness and distress; to cultivate Christian sympathy in feeling and Christian courtesy in speech....**

Paul writes to the Roman Christians, saying, **If it is possible, live peaceably with all men. Romans 12:18. Be kindly affectionate to one another with brotherly love. Romans 12:10 NKJV.** To the Ephesian Christians he wrote, **Be completely humble and gentle; be patient, bearing with one another in love. Make every effort to keep the unity of the Spirit through the bond of peace. Ephesians 4:2-3**

NIV. To the Christians in Philippi, he wrote, **...then make my joy complete by being like-minded, having the same love, being one in spirit and of one mind. Philippians 2:2 NIV.** It does not matter how much we say we love God, if we do not demonstrate love for each other, we are being disingenuous, and deserve to be called hypocrites.

A teacher asked her Sunday School class, "Why do you love God?" Several responses came forth. A man named James responded in a way that captured the attention of all: "I guess it just runs in the family." As a member of God's family, we pledge to look out for one another, pray for one another, and aid one another. We love because God first loved us. We pray because Jesus prayed for us. "It just runs in the family."

As the pastor/under-shepherd, it is impossible to provide all the pastoral care; that's why pastoral care ministries have been developed. The **Class System** which I mentioned earlier assigns members to a "class," with one member designated as the "Class Leader." The "Class Leader" contacts members at least once a month to see how each person is doing and informs them of activities and services of the church. The Class Leader notifies the pastor as to who might be sick or hospitalized. They also give death notifications and inform the pastor of those who might need special prayer or who are experiencing significant events.

In the Baptist Church, the Deacons' ministry is an extension of pastoral care. The Deacons bear the brunt of keeping in touch with the membership and informing the pastor of special needs and special events in the lives of members. Deacons minister to the spiritual and benevolent needs of the congregation in partnership with the pastor/under-shepherd of the church.

Acts Chapter 6 describes a challenge encountered by the early church and the apostles. Grecian Jewish widows complained that they were not receiving their fair share of the daily food distribution. The apostles expressed concern that any time they devoted to "waiting on tables" would take away from the time they needed to pray and preach. So, they set up a process by which seven individuals were selected to be in charge of this ministry.

From the earliest days of the church, it was clear that all pastoral care could not be provided by the pastor/under-shepherd. Churches of all denominations are moving toward developing an every-member ministry model of pastoral care, where church members are encouraged to care for one another through small groups, with the pastor/under-shepherd giving specific directions and oversight.

Many people have misunderstood the responsibility of the pastor, often thinking that the pastor's primary responsibility is preaching on Sunday. The joke that pastors work only one day a week could not be farther from the truth. In addition to preparing and delivering sermons, pastors lead Bible study, provide counseling, visit members at home and in the hospital, and serve on civic and community boards. Pastoral care is a two-way street where pastors take care of us, and we take care of our pastors.

Caring for the people of God during this pandemic has challenged the best pastoral care ministry and the most dedicated pastors/under-shepherds. We have not witnessed such a crisis in our lifetimes. It has required our best creative responses, aided by the Holy Spirit, to maintain some sense of normalcy as caretakers of God's flock.

Pre-Covid-19, at Vine Memorial Baptist Church, we were doing 6am prayer meetings Monday through Friday, Wednesday morning Bible study, followed by a noonday prayer meeting with a message by myself or one of the associates, repeating the order on Wednesday evening. Once the pandemic hit, we were tossed into the middle of the "digital highway." Our Media Ministry Coordinator suddenly died during the latter half of March 2020 and left us with little or no understanding of what to do. Two of the members were able to stream our Sunday service via Facebook and through the church's website until we added Zoom about five months into the pandemic. We began using the teleconference line for Bible Study and prayer meeting. I had the audacity to add 8pm evening prayers Monday through Friday. Each evening, I would share pertinent information including deaths and recognizing members' birthdays. With an older congregation that was, for the most part, ill- equipped for this digital age, I realized that to further coalesce the congregation I needed to do a newsletter . What a daunting time!

While it has been demanding, it has also been overwhelmingly rewarding and encouraging. To be with family members by conference call or at a graveside, physically distanced service has meant so much in their difficult times. Life-long bonds have developed because of such expressed care and concern between pastor and families. When I called members to wish them a "Happy Birthday" from Paula and myself, the excitement and joy from the celebrant was as if I had given them a hundred dollars in gold. One person said that the busy pastor taking time out to remember them "made my day."

Maya Angelou was spot-on when she said: *"I've learned that people will forget what you said, people will forget what you did, but people will never forget how you made them feel."*

Many and varied are the duties and responsibilities of a pastor as set forth by the denominational hierarchy and local congregation. The driving force behind pastoral care is empathy. The word *pastor* comes from the Latin word for *shepherd*. A pastor is to be a shepherd, a caretaker of God's flock. Pastoral care is the one thing that people associate with the church. Expressing care and concern for one another has been a part of the Christian faith since the beginning. The challenge in this "high tech world" is to be equally "high touch." Know that I am praying for you and your ministry. Do not grow weary in caring!

Ralph E Blanks, Pastor
Vine Memorial Baptist Church
Philadelphia, PA 19131

PILLAR 4

Stewardship

By Bishop Steven M. Arnold

THE BIBLE REMINDS US IN Genesis 8:22 that "While the earth remaineth, seedtime and harvest....shall not cease." While I have referenced this text many times in sermons and lessons, I still wonder if the Body of Christ has grasped the concept of Stewardship.

Stewardship is more than a process to receive physical blessings. It's how we handle the blessings we receive. As we dig into the concept of Stewardship, we see from Scripture that this concept is as old as humanity. As a matter of fact, the first gift God gave to man was not woman, but the title of Steward. "The LORD God took the man and put him in the Garden of Eden to work it and take care of it. And the LORD God commanded the man, 'You are free to eat from any tree in the garden; but you must not eat from the tree of the knowledge of good and evil, for when you eat from it you will certainly die.'" (Genesis 2:15-17 NLT).

That which man interpreted as a command from God was really a job. What God was trying to get Adam (and us) to understand was that, before I can receive the blessing, I must learn the lesson of Stewardship. God has every resource the local church needs to survive and thrive. As leaders, we need to understand the **first lesson of blessings**:

Stewardship Comes Before the Blessing

The next lesson regarding Stewardship in the local church is:

Demonstration Comes Before Communication

As the local church, it is our responsibility to demonstrate the concept of tithing. Scripture reminds us that "a tithe of everything…belongs to the Lord" (Lev. 27:30). Since the word "tithe" means the tenth part of something, a tithe is a tenth of the whole of…anything. As churches collect resources in the forms of service and finances, these gifts should come from a tenth of the whole of the members. But how do we demonstrate this concept to the congregations? It has been my experience that tithing as a church not only blesses the church, but it also gives a corporate example of an individual concept. It should be the church's responsibility to take 10% of their financial resources and tithe. Those finds can go to servicing the community or toward a cause that the church agrees on. The concept of corporate tithing as it relates to stewardship should be communicated to the congregation and EVERY BLESSING that the church receives should be celebrated because of church tithing. Don't just tell them—show them.

The last lesson of stewardship is:

Stewardship Begins with Leadership

As leaders in the local church, specifically Senior and Lead Pastors, we should be in the top tier of givers. Luke 12:48 says in essence, to whom much is given, much is required. Leadership is more than being able to park in the prime parking spot or being served by members. Leadership is about service. What better way to serve the local body of believers than to sow with a generous heart? As we look at churches that are blessed, we see one common denominator, a leader that is a great steward…of people and resources. We cannot expect to lead God's house if we cannot lead our own houses. Generosity is just as contagious as a smile. The difference between the two is one is external and the other is internal. People see our smile, but they feel our hearts. True Stewardship is about the condition of our heart. Let's remember these three principles of local church stewardship:

1. Stewardship Comes Before the Blessing
2. Demonstration Comes Before Communication
3. Stewardship Begins with Leadership

If we as leaders keep these lessons at the forefront of our work in the local church, there is indeed a blessing from the Lord.

PILLAR 5

Temple Maintenance

"...ZEAL for God's House Consumes Me..."
(Psalm 69:9; John 2:17)
By Rev. Dr. Donna Jones

THE WORD "HOUSE" IN PSALM 69:9 and John 2:17 can mean many things. It could refer to the household of God for instance, or it could refer to the physical Temple itself, including: its structure, function, and significance to God, and to God's Creation. Fortunately for us, our God continuously provides aiding physical structures for our Creator's Divine Ecology.

The ecological Society of America defines Ecology as the study of the relationships between living organisms and their physical environment.[7] This science reminds us to remember

---

7   Ecological Society of America, "What is Ecology". Accessed 31 July 2021, https://www.esa.org/about/what-does-ecology-have-to-do-with-me/.

the purposes and benefits these vital interconnections and how we and our posterity can utilize these resources in ways that sustain everyone's-, and everything's-, overall health and wellbeing for generations into the future. Jesus reminds us of the simplicity of this God-designed interconnectedness.

In Matthew 6 Jesus invites us to "Consider the Lilies – how they grow"? We ourselves know that they require an in-ground *structure*, provided by God for their support and sustenance. In the same text, Jesus adds: "Behold the birds of the air…". Those very birds, free in flight, have received a physical bodily structure that works in concert with the material, unseen. structures of the air permitting their seemingly effortless flight across the heavens. God's wisdom graciously provides structural beauty throughout creation and, in trust, invites us to join into our Lord's creative inspirations.

As I prepared to write this essay, I was struck by an often-recurring theme. Do we invest in the care, maintenance, beautification, and or expansion of these church structures of ours? Is the "building fund", languishing in bank, being depleted by every non-structural need of the people? Have we done away completely with special emphasis, special days, special activities, special offerings, special… traditions that create an overall ecology of care for our physical plants? Every now and then we preach a sermon about feet – those appendages that carry the weight of our personal physical structure that, if ignored, cause devastation across our entire lifestyle.

The below conversation led me to wonder if this chapter of the book would even be read – or, just skipped over in favor of culturally popular missions that impact and sustain congregational life and development.

Why begin talking about the science of Ecology? This musing began during a recent ZOOM conversation with a friend during which I recognized a continuously resurrecting trend amongst church-folk. Do we even need these costly, seemingly burdensome, designated congregational formal spaces? Let's listen in to the opening sentence of that conversation with my clergy friend during the reflective season of *COVID-Tide*.

Friend: "My Members are finally seeing that our Church building is a waste of money. I hope we never go back. We should sell our buildings and use the money to benefit the community!" Yes, this Pastoral colleague experienced a particular enlightenment that day.

I experienced dismay.

The sentiment that the crisis of Covid created an opportunity to pour new wines into new skins sounded so fresh and progressive to so many members of The Body of Christ this season. Perhaps you too have engaged in these historically progressive conversations, during which you and your own colleagues expressed epiphanies related to every aspect of our institutional lives together in community, including: our liturgies, outreach, teaching, preaching, chaplaincy, and of course: those buildings. A quote from Christianity Today from our recent past - 2009:

> *"It is our consumer-mentality that causes us to think we need buildings. Buildings can be great tools, but the Church gets by...no, the church thrives...every day without them."*[8]

---

[8] Ken Eastburn, "Wrong About Church Buildings 2: A Response to Dan Kimball," Christianity Today, December 2009, accessed 31 July 2021, https://www.christianitytoday.com/pastors/2009/december-online-only/wrong-about-church-buildings-2.html.

Unquestionably "...there is nothing new under the sun". There's a historic and repetitive temptation ever inflicting clergy and congregations throughout the ages to dispose of anything seemingly administratively bothersome because of a recurring and expected hope toward ushering in a Spiritual Renewal by jettisoning all things sensate. Thus, freeing *The Body* to minister without these earthly constructed constraints.

The timely epiphany that inevitably follows such reflections becomes: "Does not progressive Stewardship of God's resources demand that we loosen the restrictive bonds of maintenance, property development, and beautification in favor of direct investment in people and their communities?" Therefore, this essay about facilities and maintenance, invites us to first acknowledge those hidden whispers of weariness coercing our extrication from the often-daunting demands sounding forth from our seemingly big-budget and labor-intensive physical plants?

Perhaps these ever renewed, albeit millennially old, conversations about the necessity of buildings reflect an ancient, often exasperating, and sometimes institutionally driven thorn in our congregational side. Preparation for unpacking these expressions may invite us to search deep within our own to explore our own traditions. Then we can count the cost, and ask – "is it worth it"?

Spoiler alert: my answer? – yes!

Let's explore together three considerations: 1) mission of the edifice; 2) care for the edifice; 3) worth *from* the edifice.

#1: Mission of the Edifice.

Mission-directed physical assets, such as church edifices, provide impactful canvases for expressions of love as congregations live into, and foster, the grace that inevitably follows any act of hospitality within God's Ecosystem of intertwining Holy People and Holy Things. In reflecting on their own ministry of Stewardship, Van Tatenhove and Mueller foundationally state an essential theological premise that informs incarnational mission: "Church buildings belong ultimately to God".

> *"Rather than focusing on the burden of their upkeep, we focus on our renewed belief that God has fresh purposes we are only beginning to glimpse.*[9]

They remind us that stewarding these physical assets advance God's Kingdom and position our congregation in ministry with and on behalf of current and future generation. The authors challenge us to discern together how we can make these Divine ecosystems of physical and human resources a powerhouse for mission. They caution us to always recognize this truth: that all of these assets belong to God: not to the name(s) on the deed, the Pastor, or the Trustees.

A few truths we already know about God's purpose in physical assets.

---

[9] Van Tatenhove Krin and Mueller Rob. Neighborhood Church: Transforming Your Congregation into a Powerhouse for Mission. Westminster John Knox Press, 2019.

a) They connect us with the people that God sends our way.

This fact never ceases to amaze me in its simplicity. Last week, I pulled up to the church and began to inventory my belongings while inside the car. Computer case? – yes. Phone? – yes. Keys? – yes. I reached for the door and experienced an unexpected intrusion. A young adult had ridden up beside me on a bike, stopped and stood between me and the front walk with a surgical mask covering their chin only. I breathed as I was politely greeted first. The unexpected neighbor proclaimed simply – "I see your going into this church, Miss – I want to be Baptized. Do ya'll Baptize?"

Let us review I had not preached any powerful sermon. No lyric choir in perfect pitch had sung a beloved Song of Zion. I had not even smiled in a way that invites welcome. I had even backed up, do to COVID restrictions. I did absolutely nothing right to express Biblical Hospitality. Yet, this young adult felt a welcome. Lord knows, it didn't come from me. I remembered the ancient text – "And I, when I am lifted up from the earth, will draw all people unto myself" (John 12:32 NIV). This young adult fulfilled the vow made to God before I even knew of the person's existence. Wow! God's love and presence had spoken first from the very rocks of our building – spoking directly to that young saint!

The purpose of the church? To be the visible expression of God's loving presence in the community.

After this wonderful conversation with a new friend and future congregant, I entered the Church: struck by the beauty of the altar, the windows, the Sanctuary. I knelt and thanked

God for the altar cushions, the neighbor's introduction, and for the new relationship (sustained to this day). I thanked God for our building and for all of those who lovingly care for it daily. I thanked God for the Churches' Witness - even when "closed". I thanked God that the encounter happened with ease, because on that particular day – this particular Pastor was tired!

Funny how those scriptures memorized during a Sunday School class, in a room holding this Child of God a half of a century ago – "For My yoke is easy and My burden is [indeed] light" (Matthew 11:30) continues to Speak to me from within another Church's Stones today. There are so many ways these Churches themselves "preach" even when we don't, won't, or can't: reminding those inside, and those walking pass, that: "God has moved into the neighborhood" (John 1:14 The Message).

Sober Reminder: Familiarity breeds contempt. How often have we missed hearing God's voice – especially when inevitably the roof falls into the Altar; the steam pipes boiler burst damaging the ebony and the ivory; the toilet's water overflows onto the newly carpeted hallway, or the instruments become permanently discordant.

At times, our familiarity with the physical and financial strain of upkeep stops up our ears from hearing the still small voice of God speaking out from the stones. I propose that contempt envelopes us, our congregations, and our trustees, bred not from familiarity alone, but from unfamiliarity with maintenance. Now that breeds contempt!

#2: Care of the Edifice

How do we spell ministry? W.O.R.C. Pronounced ("Work"). **W**ork **O**n **R**estoring and **C**reating. Pastors and Congregations together must remain vigilant toward maintaining the outward and inward elements of our campuses. In addition to wood, stone, instruments, furniture, flooring, and other visible materials; we must also maintain, replace, and repair the vital inner operating structures (eg: electrical, plumbing, etc.) and civil services (utilities) that support the ministry.

Do not neglect the discipline of sustaining a professional maintenance plan, with scheduled review and evaluation on-foot, and on-paper. Sadly, insurance claims following storm damage have been denied because the scheduled maintenance, demanded by the physical resource's creators, were neglected, or ignored.

Teach the congregation to remain alert and to report damaged tiles, flaking paint, areas of moisture, signs of unwelcome creatures, great and small. Likewise, make reporting physical plant concerns to the appropriate leadership a part of your congregations culture. Some congregations have forms placed in readily accessible locations throughout the buildings. These forms regularly collected and reviewed by Trustees and building maintenance teams. (This is not a scriptural reference, but a truth from our grandparents: "A stitch in time, safes nine".)

Utilize licensed and insured contractors, clean the gutters, know the building's foundation, and immediately address signs of weakness or damage. Regularly check for wear; weather damage; cracks; fissures; dripping faucets; leaking pipes; worn wires; cracks and potholes in walkways and parking lots. Check sound, telecommunication, and musical technology. Train all the buildings occupants and leadership to fill out and turn-in these reports.

The Good News! God provides for everything needed: a) affordable church maintenance software packages, b) Charitable Foundations that specialize in assisting congregations to repair and sustain sacred spaces, and c) skilled volunteers.

True Story: Our church soup kitchen presented our small congregation with a human resource challenge. We needed help! We reached out to a friendly sister-congregation to supplement our outreach team one day a month and carryout the preparation, serving, and clean-up duties on that day. The congregation responded enthusiastically, and faithfully handled everything one Friday per month for five years, never missing a day.

Once, during on retreat together, we had an in-prompt-to opportunity to discuss individual occupations. We discovered that the outreach team, relieving us every Friday, all participated in a mission group specializing in building projects. We learned that their team's occupations included, carpenters, electricians, plumbers, and building engineers! Who knew!??? We had major lay-maintenance work identified during a routine building inspection. We immediately removed these "tool-men" from soup-detail and recruited them to assist our trustees one day per month in developing and implement our building maintenance plan. This relationship continued for over 10 years.

Moral – we never know the diamonds God has placed in our midst. Strive to have a formal skill inventory system for members and volunteers! Build relationships with other churches, training schools, community residents, and local contractors. In this way, you will experience joyful amazement at how many neighbors will pitch in for a few pieces of fried chicken and fellowship in order to assist your team in reasonable building maintenance and repairs. Lastly, do not neglect families and individuals who have left the fellowship, but welcome sustaining friendship.

#3: Worth from the edifice

While in Seminary, I visited congregations who included ministry space partnerships in their mission strategies. Congregations welcomed smaller churches to share space, Day Care Centers, Social Service agencies, small private schools, scout troops, neighborhood clubs and sports associations. These congregation with vision for building-ministry recognized these organizations as "Partners" in ministry, rather than "tenants". In this way, congregations with few children became places of renewal with childish laughter and energy. Also, communities developing new identities and relationships, found neutral spaces within which to vision new neighborhoods and cement new neighbors. Likewise, congregations with green spaces became community gardens sustaining health and building social capital, while exchanging recipes with neighbors and contributing to God's natural eco-system.

Last story:

For over 150 years my congregation occupied its own building. A beautiful, traditional edifice on a busy corner of a changing neighborhood in our city. Various factors, related to economics and migration of neighbors and members caused us to leave the cherished facility. We determined to rent space within a similarly structured church across town. The new facility had a gym, a great kitchen, fellowship halls, stage, and classrooms. The small congregation that sustained the facility had adopted a mission plan that emphasized hospitality. They intentionally invited a daycare, a new community-developed non-profit, and our church to join them as partners in ministry.

During the first year – our congregation wanted to have a formal Christmas pageant. Our host congregation had no formal children's ministry. We had over a dozen children and a children's ministry. At a regularly scheduled Partner's Meeting, we discussed our hope for a Christmas Pageant. Our hosts face lit up with excitement.

They already had dozens of costumes and a formal script that presented a wonderful opportunity for adults and children to engage the Christmas Story together. They welcomed our entire squad to participate, and together adults and children alike became transformed in ways neither church could have done alone. During the play, as the shepherds watched over their human sheep, and a reluctant young Mary and Joseph processed carrying a very much alive and uncomfortable baby Jesus – the sanctuary itself lit up beyond its natural light. I truly believe God laughed and cried with us at the beautiful sight. Such a Joy!

Do we need our buildings? Yes, they remain a wonderous part of our Lord's Ecosystem: nourishing, engaging, enlivening, and celebrating all the assets God provided and set in motion to work together in productive unity before the very foundations of the world – declaring the presence and Glory of God.

PILLAR 6

Christian Fellowship

Biblical Concept Of Fellowship
By Rev. Dr. Gerald Parker, Sr.

JESUS PRAYED FOR OUR FELLOWSHIP: "I do not ask for these only, but also for those who will believe in me through their word, *that they may all be one,* just as you, Father, are in me, and I in you, *that they may be one in us,* so that the world may believe that thou hast sent me" (John 17:20-21).

It should be noted that Jesus prayed that we might be one. The High Priestly prayer of Jesus features three sections. In the first section, Jesus prays for himself:

(John 17:1-5) [1]"These words spake Jesus, and lifted up his eyes to heaven, and said, Father, the hour is come; glorify thy Son, that thy Son also may glorify thee: [2]As thou hast given him power over all flesh, that he should give eternal life to as many as thou hast given him. [3]And this is life eternal, that they might know thee the only true God, and Jesus Christ, whom thou hast sent. [4]I have glorified thee on the earth: I have finished the work which thou gavest me to do. [5]And now, O Father, glorify thou me with thine own self with the glory which I had with thee before the world was."

In the second section, Jesus prays for His first disciples:

(John 17:6-19) [6]I have manifested thy name unto the men which thou gavest me out of the world: thine they were, and thou gavest them me; and they have kept thy word. [7]Now they have known that all things whatsoever thou hast given me are of thee. [8]For I have given unto them the words which thou gavest me; and they have received *them*, and have known surely that I came out from thee, and they have believed that thou didst send me. [9]I pray for them: I pray not for the world, but for them which thou hast given me; for they are thine. [10]And all mine are thine, and thine are mine; and I am glorified in them. [11]And now I am no more in the world, but these are in the world, and I come to thee. Holy Father, keep through thine own name those whom thou hast given me, that they may be one, as we *are*. [12]While I was with them in the world, I kept them in thy name: those that thou gavest me I have kept, and none of them is lost, but the son of perdition; that the scripture might be fulfilled. [13]And now come I to thee; and these things I speak in the world, that they might have my joy fulfilled in themselves. [14]I have given them thy word; and the world hath hated them, because they are not of the world, even as I am not of the world. [15]I pray not that thou shouldest take them out of the world, but that thou shouldest keep them from the evil. [16]They are not of the world, even as I am not of the world. ¹⁷Sanctify them through thy truth: thy word is truth. ¹⁸As thou hast sent me into the world, even so have I also sent them into the world. ¹⁹And for their sakes I sanctify myself, that they also might be sanctified through the truth.

In the final section, Jesus prays for those who will believe in Him through the Words of the original disciples. He prays for those disciples who did not see Him during His earthly ministry. In other words, Jesus prays for us. What does Jesus pray for regarding us?

1. Our unity
2. Our fellowship.

In (John 17:20-23), Jesus prays three times that we might be one. He prays to the Father that we live in unity and oneness.

(John 17:20-23) ¹⁷Sanctify them through thy truth: thy word is truth. ¹⁸As thou hast sent me into the world, even so have I also sent them into the world. ¹⁹And for their sakes I sanctify myself, that they also might be sanctified through the truth. ²⁰Neither pray I for these alone, but for them also which shall believe on me through their word; ²¹That they all may be one; as thou, Father, *art* in me, and I in thee, that they also may be one in us: that the world may believe that thou hast sent me. ²²And the glory which thou gavest me I have given them; that they may be one, even as we are one: ²³I in them, and thou in me, that they may be made perfect in one; and that the world may know that thou hast sent me, and hast loved them, as thou hast loved me.

Christ prayed for the unity of the church. Many of our local assemblies certainly need prayer for unity and fellowship. Christ's prayer is however a prayer for the fellowship of all believers. Most local churches will not have unity because they are filled with unbelievers.

This is a spiritual fellowship and not a physical or materialistic fellowship. It is not a fellowship of ritual. It is a unity with God the Father and God the Son. The results of this fellowship will enhance our witness. It will help evangelism.

When the church begins to demonstrate fellowship and unity, the world is hit by an inescapable impression that Jesus is Lord.

When I was a boy, we used to sing a song at church entitled "What a Fellowship". Now that I am old, I realize that many people were singing that song without knowing what fellowship was.

I personally believe that Christian Fellowship is the most vital pillar of the church.

I believe that the purpose of the church is THREE-fold.

1. **Exalt Christ** – (Psalm 150)
   [1]Praise ye the LORD. Praise God in his sanctuary: praise him in the firmament of his power. [2]Praise him for his mighty acts: praise him according to his excellent greatness. [3]Praise him with the sound of the trumpet: praise him with the psaltery and harp.

⁴Praise him with the timbrel and dance: praise him with stringed instruments and organs. ⁵Praise him upon the loud cymbals: praise him upon the high sounding cymbals. ⁶Let every thing that hath breath praise the LORD. Praise ye the Lord

2. **Edify the Saints** – (John 13:34)
   ³⁴A new commandment I give unto you, That ye love one another; as I have loved you, that ye also love one another.

3. **Evangelize the Sinners** (Acts 1:8)
   ⁸But ye shall receive power, after that the Holy Ghost is come upon you: and ye shall be witnesses unto me both in Jerusalem, and in all Judaea, and in Samaria, and unto the uttermost part of the earth.

In order for a church to accomplish her three-fold purpose, fellowship must be experienced in the church.

In 1 Corinthians 12:27 we learn that the church is the body of Christ, and each believer is a working member. In order for the body to accomplish her purpose there must be unity and fellowship among the members.

(1 Corinthians 12:27) ²⁷*Now ye are the body of Christ, and members in particular.*

What Fellowship Is Not

In order to understand what fellowship is, it is helpful to see what it is not, and what passes for fellowship is not true fellowship.

Real fellowship is not eating food, not sharing in a meal with other Christians. This may be a great environment for true fellowship, but food is not essential.

Real fellowship is not sharing different opinions. Too often the exchange of opinions is more like a forum for people to simply say what is on their minds instead of fellowship.

Today's churches have fellowship halls, fellowship dinners, and fellowship retreats, but very few have real fellowship.

What Fellowship Is

Let's look at what is the biblical meaning of fellowship.

The New Testament word for fellowship is *"Koinonia."* It expresses the idea of being together for mutual benefits.

(Hebrew 10:24-28) *[24]And let us consider one another to provoke unto love and to good works: [25]Not forsaking the assembling of ourselves together, as the manner of some is; but exhorting one another: and so much the more, as ye see the day approaching. [26]For if we sin wilfully after that we have received the knowledge of the truth, there remaineth no more sacrifice for sins, [27]But a certain fearful looking for of judgment and fiery indignation, which shall devour the adversaries. [28]He that despised Moses' law died without mercy under two or three witnesses:*

We see that the root of the word fellowship means to hold something in common for the same purpose. This idea of fellowship means having things in common, because we share things in common with each other. We have:

1. **Same God**
   (Ephesians 4:6) *⁶One God and Father of all, who is above all, and through all, and in you all.*

2. **Common Salvation**
   (Jude 3) *³Beloved, when I gave all diligence to write unto you of the common salvation, it was needful for me to write unto you, and exhort you that ye should earnestly contend for the faith which was once delivered unto the saints.*

3. **Common Faith**
   (Titus 1:4) *⁴To Titus, mine own son after the common faith: Grace, mercy, and peace, from God the Father and the Lord Jesus Christ our Saviour,* and in Acts – all things in common.
   (Acts 2:44) *⁴⁴And all that believed were together, and had all things common;*
   (Acts 4:32) *³²And the multitude of them that believed were of one heart and of one soul: neither said any of them that ought of the things which he possessed was his own; but they had all things common.*

When The Bible Talks About Fellowship It Refers To:

1. **Shared life from Jesus**
   Sometimes the word fellowship is used to explain the bond between believers and the Lord.
   (1 Corinthians 1:9) *⁹God is faithful, by whom ye were called unto the fellowship of his Son Jesus Christ our Lord.*

2. **Shared life with each other**
   Fellowship also involves the ways believers help one another, often in the context of meeting physical needs. (Hebrews 13:16) *16But to do good and to communicate forget not: for with such sacrifices God is well pleased.*

3. **Shared living for the same purpose**
   (Acts 2 :42-44) *42And they continued steadfastly in the apostles' doctrine and fellowship, and in breaking of bread, and in prayers. 43And fear came upon every soul: and many wonders and signs were done by the apostles 44And all that believed were together, and had all things common;*

Why Is Fellowship So Important?

1. **Fellowship gives us a picture of God.**
   Each of us together shows all of God's graces to the world. Each of us has been given specific spiritual gifts, when we use these gifts together, we show the glory of God.
   (Romans 12:4-6) *4For as we have many members in one body, and all members have not the same office: 5So we, being many, are one body in Christ, and every one members one of another. 6Having then gifts differing according to the grace that is given to us, whether prophecy, let us prophesy according to the proportion of faith;*

2. **Fellowship makes us stronger**
   No matter where we are in our faith, fellowship provides us with strength. Being around other believers gives us the chance to learn and grow in faith.
   (Matthew 18:19-20) *[19]Again I say unto you, That if two of you shall agree on earth as touching any thing that they shall ask, it shall be done for them of my Father which is in heaven. [20]For where two or three are gathered together in my name, there am I in the midst of them.*

3. **Fellowship Provides Encouragement**
   We all have had moments, whether it's a loss of a loved one, a failed examination, money problems, or even a crisis of faith where we can find ourselves down. Spending time with other believers can often lift us up.
   (Hebrew 10:24-25) *[24]And let us consider one another to provoke unto love and to good works: [25]Not forsaking the assembling of ourselves together, as the manner of some is; but exhorting one another: and so much the more, as ye see the day approaching.*

4. **Fellowship reminds us we are not alone and that we need each other**
   (1 Corinthians 12:21) *[21]And the eye cannot say unto the hand, I have no need of thee: nor again the head to the feet, I have no need of you.*

5. **Fellowship helps us grow**
   Coming together is a great way for each of us to grow in our faith. When we come together in fellowship we teach each other things.
   (1 Corinthians 14:26) *²⁶How is it then, brethren? when ye come together, every one of you hath a psalm, hath a doctrine, hath a tongue, hath a revelation, hath an interpretation. Let all things be done unto edifying.*

6. **Fellowship helps us carry on the will and purpose of God**
   Since we are the body of Christ, when we come together in fellowship, we carry out God's plan and purpose in the world.
   (Acts 1:8) *⁸But ye shall receive power, after that the Holy Ghost is come upon you: and ye shall be witnesses unto me both in Jerusalem, and in all Judaea, and in Samaria, and unto the uttermost part of the earth.*
   (Ephesians 3:8-11) *⁸Unto me, who am less than the least of all saints, is this grace given, that I should preach among the Gentiles the unsearchable riches of Christ; ⁹And to make all men see what is the fellowship of the mystery, which from the beginning of the world hath been hid in God, who created all things by Jesus Christ: ¹⁰To the intent that now unto the principalities and powers in heavenly places might be known by the church the manifold wisdom of God, ¹¹According to the eternal purpose which he purposed in Christ Jesus our Lord:*

7. **Fellowship is the heartbeat of your congregation**
   Simply stated, it is the life of the church family. Fellowship may not be the church, but it is why they stay.
   People who are church hunting will list a dozen things they are looking for in their next place of worship. But more than anything else, what they are looking for is fellowship.

8. **Fellowship is a powerfull witness to the world**
   A unified church is one of the strongest evidences of the truth of the gospel. When the rest of the world can't seem to agree on anything or bear to be around people who are different, a church where natural enemies become siblings in Christ is a powerful witness. Fellowship is a critical manifestation of a spirit-empowered church.
   This is why Paul told the Ephesian Christians to be "eager to maintain the unity of the spirit in the bond of peace."
   (Ephesians 4:3) *3Endeavouring to keep the unity of the Spirit in the bond of peace.*

It's why he wrote to the Corinthians: "I appeal to you, brothers by the name of our Lord Jesus Christ, that all you agree and that there be no divisions among you, but that you be united in the same mind and the same judgment."

(Corinthians 1:10) *[10]Now I beseech you, brethren, by the name of our Lord Jesus Christ, that ye all speak the same thing, and that there be no divisions among you; but that ye be perfectly joined together in the same mind and in the same judgment.*

Jesus said, "By this all people will know that you are my disciple. If you love one another."

(John 13:35) *³⁵By this shall all men know that ye are my disciples, if ye have love one to another.*

We cannot expect the world to believe that the Father sent his Son, that Jesus' claims are true, and that Christianity is true, unless the world sees the reality of the fellowship of the church.

ADDENDUM: More detailed information on Fellowship as an important pillar of the church.

Is there real Christian fellowship in your church? A church can never be vibrant without fellowship.
(Acts 2 :41-47) gives us the necessary ingredients for real Christian fellowship.

1. The world must be preached and received.
   (Acts 2:44) *44And all that believed were together, and had all things common;*

2. There must be baptized believers in Jesus Christ.
   (Acts 2:41) *41Then they that gladly received his word were baptized: and the same day there were added unto them about three thousand souls.*

3. The word of God must be steadfastly taught.
   (Acts 2:42) *[42]And they continued steadfastly in the apostles' doctrine and fellowship, and in breaking of bread, and in prayers.*
   Every pastor should seek to be unoriginal in the sense that we don't have our own doctrine but the apostles' doctrine.

4. The membership must be zealous about Bible Study.
   (Acts 2:42) *[42]And they continued steadfastly in the apostles' doctrine and fellowship, and in breaking of bread, and in prayers.*

5. Fellowship will take place when the membership study God's word together.
   a) The Christian life is meant to be full of fellowship, of sharing with one another.
      - We share the same Lord.
      - We share the same guide for life.
      - We share the same love for God.
      - We share the same desire to worship Him.
      - We share in our walk with Jesus.

      (1 John 1:7) *[7]But if we walk in the light, as he is in the light, we have fellowship one with another, and the blood of Jesus Christ his Son cleanseth us from all sin.*

6. Fellowship will take place when people pray together. Everything else we read about the power and glory of the early church flows from the foundation of the word, prayer, and breaking of bread together.

Remember: Christians have an ongoing affair with the word of God. We meditate on the word, we memorize the word, and we model the word. We have fellowship because of the word.

7. Fellowship is definitely a Vital Pillar.
We need to strive to keep the fellowship.
(Ephesians 4:3) *³Endeavouring to keep the unity of the Spirit in the bond of peace.*

PILLAR 7

The Ministry of Worship

By Rev. Larry D. James

LET ME BEGIN BY SAYING that I am humbled by the invitation from Reverend William Thrasher, my longtime friend, high school classmate, and ministry colleague, to participate in this project of *Seven Pastors Responding to the Seven Pillars for Successful Service*.

This work is not intended to be an academic substitute for formal training in the pastoral and church ministry. William offers his handbook as an account of the personal experience he gained as a pastor. He learned the vocation up close and personal, with minimal mentorship from seasoned practitioners in pastoral ministry.

What I will attempt to offer to new pastors is a practical approach to engaging a congregation in the area of **worship**. This information is derived from my thirty years of pastoral ministry in small to mid-size congregations. Though I attended seminary and received a Master of Divinity degree, there were many things I encountered for which seminary did not and could not prepare me.

For the purpose of this rendering, the focus will be uniquely on **Christian worship**. That said, there is a plethora of religious and spiritual institutions that practice various forms of worship. They all have as their object of devotion a deity of a higher source of power. Those sources of power may bear a variety of names, shapes, and symbols. Nevertheless, they all elicit devotion and commitment from their particular worshippers. As a beginning point of discussion, let us define worship.

Webster's Dictionary defines worship as, (1) the feeling or expression of reverence for a deity, (2) showing reverence and adoration for a deity through the practice of religious rites, (3) reverence paid to a supernatural or divine being. Etymologically, the Old English term worship is in the compound form, *woert*-worth, and *scipe*-ship = worth-ship. Essentially, the meaning equates to being worthy. Thus, the object of devotion in Christianity is God, who is worthy of the worshipper's commitment and reverence.

Typically, the word worship is used in both noun and verb forms. The word is used interchangeably with terms and expressions like, **church service, having church**, and often bespeaks an activity done in a particular place at designated times. The activity is comprised of rituals, symbolisms, and signs with an expectation of an emotional and subdued conclusion. Each congregation develops its own logic and then functions in ways particular to that group. In other words, each group has its own identity, its own DNA.

Quite often, the term worship is spoken of as an outward activity of expression that occurs in/at the church building. The characterization describes a religious activity that we **do** more than who we **are** as the Church (the Called Out). When spoken in that frame of reference, we tend to minimize the internal abode of the Holy Spirit within us, upon whom worship is predicated. Thus, true worship is not time and place controlled. Whether we are in/at the church building, singing, praying, or serving, or we are living our life at work, at home, or in recreation, worshipping God should be a natural extension of everything we **do** as a result of who we **are** as God worshippers.

As earlier stated, every congregation, like each person, has DNA, its own set of characteristics that must be recognized. **That set of characteristics must be understood before criticizing it or making attempts to substantially change it.** It is a healthy exercise for pastors to assess the level of spiritual development within the congregation, realizing that the act of worship is ushered in and up from within each worshipper.

A common mistake made by many new pastors is to assume they know what the congregation needs before the needs have been assessed. First-time/new pastors must learn the art of **listening more and talking less.** Additionally, pastors generally assume the posture that as leader of the congregation they have the answers. NEWS FLASH! **You are not their pastor until they allow you to be.** *You bear the title but not the power!* Learn the congregation before trying to lead them. Get to know the culture, traditions, and sacred cows in the congregation before you attempt to make wholesale changes. Remember, worship is universal, but styles of worship vary from one congregation to another. Different is not wrong. Worship styles are like crayons: they come in a variety of expressions.

When referring to congregational worship styles, they are generally described as **conservative** or **progressive** in practice. In conservative congregations, the worship is highly ritualistic and liturgical in nature and often referred to as "High Church." Pastors wear vestments, banners are displayed, and paraments drape the podiums. Lay speakers address the congregation from a separate podium. The preaching is typically lecture styled and sermons are generally twelve to fifteen minutes in length. The music is more traditionally presented by trained chorale voices who are more prone to hymns and anthems. Handclapping and verbal shouts of response to music and preaching are rare to nonexistent. Gospel music is rarely if ever a part of the worship order. All the essentials of worship i.e., prayer, sacraments of baptism and communion are relatively solemn.

Conversely, in progressive congregations, the worship is most often guided by church programs/bulletins but may flow freely without an ordered movement. The preaching may vary in styles from lecture to storytelling accompanied by music. The sermons may be as little as twenty minutes and as long as forty-five minutes. The music can vary from traditional hymns and anthems to gospels and spirituals.

Many progressive congregations have adopted the **"praise and worship"** team concept as a means of preparing the congregation for the worship experience. Handclapping and congregational singing are encouraged, even if there is a choir or ensemble. Tambourines, drums, guitars, and keyboards are quite prevalent in these congregations. Prayer, sacraments of baptism and communion are practiced and generally solemn in nature. Unlike the conservatives, progressive congregations may from time to time solicit personal testimonies from worshippers in the context of worship.

This writer does not attempt to provide information about **Temple Maintenance**, which will be thoroughly covered by a separate contributor. However, from the worship perspective, I would offer this for consideration.

When we speak of worship, temple maintenance refers to both **the body** (human temple) and **the church building** (structural temple). In my humble opinion, in agreement with the Apostle Paul, the two are not mutually exclusive. When Spirit-filled worshippers gather for worship in the sanctuary, the sole objective is to offer up praise in response to God as **The Great Giver**. The Holy Spirit, residing in each worshipper, (human temple) enters the sanctuary (structural temple) and becomes One with God, the Holy Spirit. **Where two or more gather in Jesus' name, "there" the Spirit is in the midst** (my paraphrase).

Scripture declares that Christians have a duty to keep their bodies, which are temples of the Holy Spirit, cleansed from sin and unrighteousness. We must strive to live holy lives and avoid anything that may contaminate our bodies/temples. Equally important is our responsibility to maintain the sacred spaces within our structural temples. When we gather as the Church collectively, physical and spiritual cleanliness are the goal for fervent and holy worship.

In conclusion, I would offer five (5) recommendations for first-time pastors to consider when called to a congregation or when planting a new church.

1. Offer open-door, one-on-one, "get acquainted" meeting opportunities to get to know as many of the congregants as possible. This helps to not only give you insight into the members, but also gives them an opportunity to get acquainted with you.
2. Learn as much as you can about the history of the church and the community. Insight into this information may provide helpful knowledge in determining how you set your course for leading the congregation forward.
3. Consider the use of the **S.W.O.T** (Strengths, Weaknesses, Opportunities, and Threats) assessment tool to measure the vocational talents and spiritual maturity of the congregation. Spiritual maturity is oftentimes a direct correlation to the degree of authentic worship among the congregants.
4. Be prayerful and patient in how you engage the congregation in the area of worship. Wisdom teaches us that the ministry of worship is predicated on the spiritual growth and development of the congregation as a whole. There always exists varying degrees of spiritual growth among the membership.

    Get to know all the formal and informal leaders as much as possible before attempting to make huge changes. It has been said of first-time pastors that they too often go into congregations like "bulls in a china shop," not realizing that when prized china gets broken, the journey forward is arduous at best. Take the opportunity to teach toward the major changes that make for spiritual growth of the congregation. No matter how much education you possess from seminary or otherwise, your degree will not guarantee that your way is supreme.

5. Strive to **"Be"** the worshipper you want the congregation to "Be". **"Be-come"** the shepherd who leads the sheep with love and care. When the congregation trusts you, they will follow you. **Be** patient! **Be** humble, **Be** truthful. Rule with benevolence; take sides only with truth.

My prayer is that you will find this offering of my experiences helpful as you enter and follow the call to pastoral ministry. We generally enter into the church ministry believing that all will be joyful because we are Christians, and the love will flow among the worshippers. The great surprise and sometimes shock is that we are godly people with ungodly ways. The hope is that you will enter the call with heart, eyes, and mind open as you attempt to lead the people of God. Above all, trust God to guide you from beginning to end. *Shalom!*

Advent of Technology:

An Effective Tool in Maximizing Ministry
By Rev. Dr. D. L. Richardson

Introduction

BEFORE COVID-19 DISRUPTED THE NORMALCY of our lives, technology in the church was an option. Since the arrival of this pandemic, it is no longer an option but an obligation. What once was a choice for congregations is now a requirement. What once was eluded by many congregations must now be employed. Technology is mandatory for church survival. Even if your church is not thriving, technology is needed for it to survive. Technology in some shape, form, or fashion is a necessity.

Conquering the Fears of Technology

Although embracing technological change is a major need for the church today, it is feared by many. As the church of today embraces the future of technology, we must face the fear of change. Our mandate is too important to allow fear to hamper our efforts to advance God's kingdom. Let us look at three primary issues many of our congregations are grappling with.

One fear is the trust factor. If they don't trust it, then they won't touch it! People will never touch the button and complete an online membership application consisting of their personal information if the technology service you have in place is not trustworthy. They will never sign up for online tithing or be comfortable sharing their banking information unless they know you have a secure system in place. Yes, security plays a significant role in the integration of technology within the church. The same people who attend because they trust you, who allow you to work with their children because they trust you, who give their money because they trust you, want to know they can also trust you with their addresses, phone numbers, email addresses, and bank account information online. One security breach could destroy those all-important relationships. Make sure you eliminate the trust factor by ensuring the technological system you are utilizing, especially for membership and money, is safe and secure from all alarm.

Another fear is the talent factor. Many congregations avoid technology because of the media ministry workers' lack of knowledge. To avoid this roadblock, be willing to develop disciples of technology. Reach out to other churches that have successful media ministries and ask them to disciple your workers in the basic training needed to be effective. Give them a "Macedonia Call" and trust God to touch their hearts to say yes. The following excerpts are sample training nuggets offered by Terry Wilhite, communications and multimedia specialist, that can be rewarding in discipling technology workers. I will discuss more on the software and equipment aspect of this training in the "Calculating Your Finances" section.

You probably never imagined that you would be heading a multimedia team. Even in churches where it's only the preacher and the "sound man," that's enough to constitute a multimedia team. Regardless of your team's size, there are four key objectives that lead to seven effective practices that you should follow and teach your team to be successful. The four key objectives are:

1. It is vitally important to tell members of your multimedia team that they are more than "button pushers." They are, indeed, worship leaders. For example, if you project the lyrics of hymns on a screen, your designated multimedia specialist is the "hand" that turns the pages of the projected "hymnbook."
2. The job description includes exultation. Each team member's job is to exalt Christ, not themselves or their multimedia function.
3. Provide focus. Our goal as multimedia team members is to provide focus—that is, eliminate distractions. For example, putting the camera spotlight on the wrong subject at the wrong time can potentially divert attention away from what's happening on the main stage.
4. Be transparent. As paradoxical as it may seem with multimedia, our chief goal is to be transparent. If the sound, lighting, video, or any other multimedia element distracts from the message, team members have not been successful.

These four key goals will breed seven healthy ministry habits necessary for maximizing the efficacy of the media ministry.

1. **Communication**
   Develop a "worship service plan" that literally puts everybody on the same page.

2. **Preparation**
   Spiritual preparation should take place first, then technical preparation. Create a "preflight checklist" for each job that is performed prior to every sermon or presentation.

3. **Concentration**
   Since multimedia work usually takes place in a confined space, it's easy to become distracted by another team member's job. Each member should concentrate on *his* role and his alone.

4. **Synchronization**
   This means that the worship roster is in front of each multimedia member, eyes are focused on the stage, and hands are on the controls.

5. **Specialization**
   "Find out what you're good at and give it all you've got." One job, one function. Each person should become a specialist at his or her task.

6. **Anticipation**

    As easy as this may seem, multimedia team members must be in three places at once: the "big picture," right now, and a step ahead. If they're too late by one second while performing a task, they have caused a distraction. (Remember our goal? Transparency!)

7. **Evaluation**

    It is important for the pastor/appointee and team members to "huddle" often. None of us are perfect, but each time the gospel is communicated, it deserves our best effort.

Note that preparing a religious service involves an extensive arrangement of different elements. Utilizing a user-friendly church presentation software like Easy Worship, Pro Presenter, or Free Worship can present your message or music. These programs will help you manage all those elements from a single interface. Using these tools, you can make a detailed plan of your religious service by adding all the elements you need, from the hymns to sing, the portions of the Bible that will be read, and any other item you want to add, such as videos, audio files, PowerPoint slide shows, and more.

Microsoft PowerPoint is another powerful presentation software that can be used to create announcements. It is a standard component of the company's Microsoft Office suite software, and is bundled together with Word, Excel, and other office productivity tools. The program uses slides to convey information rich in multimedia.

To conquer the fear of talent it is not only important to have fluent knowledge of the software but also of the equipment being used, especially the audio and video equipment. Here are a few helpful audio equipment tips to aid in producing a quality sound presentation of the music and message.

- Soundboard operators should become familiar with the board and individual voices and attend choir rehearsals at times to practice board usage.
- When sound is compromised, troubleshoot the following:
  a) Make sure playback equipment like CD players, DVD players, video players, etc. are muted and not feeding back into open microphones.
  b) Make sure wireless microphone batteries are fully charged.
  c) Make sure choir microphones are not turned too high or feeding into speakers or monitors.
- Recording/Streaming operators should make sure recording/streaming levels are at a proper peak and make sure sound levels on for individual microphones are at proper peaks. Any channels for musical instruments should be at a much lower recording level so the music will not overshadow the vocal recording.

The video operation is equally as vital to the technology team as the software and audio operation. The following are helpful notes for camera usage.

- Camera operators should be in ready, set, action mode with camera on main subject when beginning rather than secondary cameras being switched from congregation to subject at the start. The less switching from congregation to stage the better, unless photogenic action is taking place in other areas.
- Using the panning and zooming features will help eliminate excessive use of non-automatic, PTZ (pivot, tilt, zoom) cameras.
- Camera operators should periodically zoom in and out on preacher during sermon to give a different look, especially when excitement is happening in the congregation. Do not substitute stage excitement for congregation excitement. It is important to feel the flow of the service to know when camera switching is needed.

Hands-on training will help to defeat the fear of talent factor in your congregation. The more knowledge and practice a person has, the more comfortable the person becomes with technology.

The third fear is the "treasure factor." Spending money on technology is not popular in many congregations and often generates an array of inquiries. *How are we going to pay for all this equipment? Do we need all of that to do kingdom work? Can we afford to purchase it?* The truth of the matter is you cannot afford *not* to purchase it. If you are going to be effective, you must become revolutionary in your church spending to remain on the cutting edge of technology. Businesses are maximizing their effectiveness through technology. Schools are maximizing their effectiveness through technology. Social organizations are maximizing their effectiveness through technology. Why not the church?

Although the concept of a media ministry budget may be new, it is needed. If your church does not have a media ministry budget for technology, then I suggest you have a discussion with your pastor or church leaders. Discuss how media fits into the overall vision and mission of the church and then develop a budget that helps to accomplish that vision and mission through the application of technology. Remember:

Conquering the fear of technology is the first step in moving forward. While technology cannot replace hugs, handshakes, or happy faces, it can provide the church with useful tools in advancing God's kingdom.

Calculating the Finances of Technology

As you cast a vision for the church of the future, make sure technology is in sight. Brainstorming, budgeting, and buying the proper software and equipment should be an intentional part of your technology plan. Begin by conducting a technology inventory assessment. Make a list of what you already have and a list of what you will need to maximize ministry through technology. For example, you may already have the computer and software to enter the giving taken up in person, but you may need additional software to access the online giving.

Another factor in calculating the finances of technology is your worship service. You may already have a sound system to project audio to in-person worshipers, but you may need additional software and equipment for online streaming.

An often overlooked calculation is the need to upgrade or replace purchased software and equipment. The moment the church installs or upgrades a new piece of technology is the moment you need to begin to save for more upgrades and eventually replacement. Technology requires maintenance, becomes outdated, and eventually wears out.

There is one more calculation that must be considered. Staff assessment and training. Will the technology be operated by volunteers only or will there be a need for paid staff? Someone must oversee and operate the technology. Even if volunteers are used, training will be needed. Don't forget to add them to the technology plan calculations.

How can you maximize ministry through technology on a small budget? It doesn't take a large budget to do effective ministry through technology. With the right equipment, the right software, and a few dedicated volunteers, you will be on your way.

In the past few years, I have been privileged to help seven congregations on a limited budget move their media ministry to the cutting edge of technology so they could be more effective. Let me share with you some starter principles.

"Teamwork makes the dream work." Create a Media and Technology team that gives church members an opportunity to use their unique skills in a way that contributes to the overall mission of the church. This will help grow your ministry team and encourage others to share the responsibility.

Take advantage of the free software that is available and the software you presently have. With a free Google account you get Google Do, which is word processing software. This and other free software like Cognito Forms can be used to create an online membership application that can be placed on your website.

It's important to focus on creating engaging and visually attractive presentations. Your church probably already has the basic $99.00 yearly Microsoft subscription or a single, purchased copy. Use Microsoft PowerPoint to create announcements and use a mobile phone or tablet to record the audio and embed it into the slide. Play it through the sound system and a computer you already have.

Free Worship is a free presentation software that provides a great way to visually convey information that otherwise may sound dry and dull. It is similar to Easy Worship and Presenter Pro, which cost about $400.00. Although its capabilities are limited, it is highly recommended for those whose budget is not ready for the aforementioned presentation software.

"How do I project the video?" For this, you will need to purchase a camera. It doesn't have to be a PTZ camera. For starters, you can purchase a Mevo All-In-One wireless live streaming camera or a similar product for under $400.00. It has the capability to live stream to Facebook, YouTube, Twitch, and many others through your internet service.

Using social media platforms like Facebook, YouTube, and Instagram to promote and present your church activities are of no cost but of great value. When moving to a new town or city, most people search for churches online before trying them out in person. These social media platforms can be used to share videos, pictures, calendars, and most of your church's activities.

Conveying Your Faith Through Technology

Technology has grown and groomed our world in many ways. Everyone from the public to the private sector is using it to communicate their products and principles. It is an integral part of today's world and should be embraced by the church. As the church seeks to maximize the effectiveness of ministry through technology, it should be viewed as a valuable resource for conveying our faith as we carry out the Great Commission.

As we take the Gospel of Jesus Christ to all the world, we must be willing to do it by any means necessary. Social media is the dominant evangelistic method of communication today. We must take advantage of this opportunity and promote the use of technology as a vital evangelistic tool.

The Church must seriously seek to become as technologically sound as possible to effectively carry out the Great Commission during these times of social isolation. The main purpose of social networking (an internet platform for communicating with one another) is to connect with other people. In the Great Commission, Jesus has given us a mandate to connect with other people: "Go ye therefore into all the world (Matt. 28:19, 20). Many strong relationships are made and matured, started and strengthened through socializing. Through social media, we can transmit information to others. What better way than social media to transmit the love of Christ to a world that sometimes looks for love in the wrong places?

Allow me to share with you a few ways in which ministry is being maximized through technology at First Baptist as we carry out the five-fold ministry of the church:

- **Celebratory Worship:** Display the song lyrics; Display the sermon topic and points; Display the Scriptures; Display the systems for giving; Display the scheduled activities.
- **Christ-centered Discipleship:** Online spiritual growth classes; Online orientation classes; Online Mid-Week Bible Study; Online Sunday School.
- **Community Evangelism:** Virtual communicating of the Gospel with one click; Virtual invitations to join the services; Virtual Revival; Virtual social networking and chatting about God's goodness and grace.
- **Christian Fellowship:** Providing opportunities for ministries to connect; Promotion of church activities; Providing potential members the opportunity to unite.

Compassionate Ministry: Social media as a tool to minister to those beyond our reach; Social media as community outreach; Social media as a promotional tool for church ministries.

CPSIA information can be obtained
at www.ICGtesting.com
Printed in the USA
LVHW051316250523
748014LV00008B/417